HYDR

Advanced Guide

The Advanced Guide to Develop the Necessary Skills to Manage an Aquaponics Growing System and Easily Grow Plants, Vegetables, and Fruits

DANIEL KING

© **Copyright 2020 by *Jack Garden*** All rights reserved.

This document is geared towards providing exact and reliable information with regards to the topic and issue covered. The publication is sold with the idea that the publisher is not required to render accounting, officially permitted, or otherwise, qualified services. If advice is necessary, legal or professional, a practiced individual in the profession should be ordered.

From a Declaration of Principles which was accepted and approved equally by a Committee of the American Bar Association and a Committee of Publishers and Associations.

In no way is it legal to reproduce, duplicate, or transmit any part of this document in either electronic means or in printed format. Recording of this publication is strictly prohibited and any storage of this document is not allowed unless with written permission from the publisher. All rights reserved.

The information provided herein is stated to be truthful and consistent, in that any liability, in terms of inattention or otherwise, by any usage or abuse of any policies, processes, or directions contained within is the solitary and utter responsibility of the recipient reader. Under no circumstances will any legal responsibility or blame be held against the publisher for any reparation, damages, or monetary loss due to the information herein, either directly or indirectly.

Respective authors own all copyrights not held by the publisher.

The information herein is offered for informational purposes solely, and is universal as so. The presentation of the information is without contract or any type of guarantee assurance.

The trademarks that are used are without any consent, and the publication of the trademark is without permission or backing by the trademark owner. All trademarks and brands within this book are for clarifying purposes only and are the owned by the owners themselves, not affiliated with this document

HYDROPONICS - by - DANIEL KING
Table Of Contents

Introduction..7

Chapter 1...13

General Hydroponics - Use Hydroponics For Better Yields..................13

Chapter 2...34

Aero Hydroponics..34

Chapter 3...46

The Secret of Master Hydroponics Producers..................................46

Chapter 4...68

Sea of Green Techniques..68

Chapter 5...95

Revolutions in Plant Cultivation..95

Conclusion..105

Introduction

Hydroponics can be briefly defined as the cultivation of plants without soil. In short, hydroponics, a Greek word meaning "hydro" (water) and "pones" (labor) is the method of growing plants in different types of substrates (chemically inert), sand, gravel, or liquid (water), in which nutrients are added, but no soil is used. Europe is considered the biggest market for hydroponics in which France, the Netherlands, and Spain are the three top producers, followed by the United States of America and the Asia-Pacific region. These systems are becoming increasingly widespread over the world, and according to the most recent report, it is expected to reach a world growth of 18.8% from 2017 to 2023, corresponding to a global hydroponic market USD 490.50 Million by 2023. According to growers, hydroponic systems help them in expanding their ability for continuous production in a short growing period, require less space, and plants can be produced anywhere, i.e., in a small space with a controlled growth environment. Growers often reply that hydroponics always allows them to have higher productivities and yields without any constrains of climate and weather conditions. Also, growers often claimed that the quality of hydroponic produces is superior because it uses a highly controlled environment and enables a more homogeneous production without any loss of water and nutrients. Moreover, hydroponics is not dependent on seasonality, and therefore, their productivities are higher and homogenous throughout the year. Growers also often report that hydroponic productions are easier, and since they do not require cultural operations such as plowing, weeding, soil fertilization, and crop rotation, they are light and clean. However, the scientific evidence is often contradictory and different disadvantages are reported to justify their rejection: high initial costs, high technical and plant physiology knowledge, periodic work routines, and efficient electrical systems. It is also necessary and effective to control nutritional solutions and take daily measurements of liquid nutrients to prevent excessive Stalinization and to combat microbial diseases and pests to prevent loss of production. However, producers often claim that this technique helps grow healthier foods and helps reduce waste. We see an example of this waste reduction in lettuce, the most hydroponic crop in the world, where around 99% of hydroponics leaves are valuable and can be sold around 40% more expensive than traditionally grown lettuce. Moreover, with hydroponics, there is a better possibility to market fresh products because their average food quality and consumer acceptance are higher. Also, producers have indicated that hydroponics avoids some negative effects of conventional agriculture, including high and inefficient water use, high land requirements, high nutrient and pesticide concentrations and soil degradation accompanied by erosion; issues that are much more in the current concerns of consumers. Consumers around the world are increasingly interested in more environmentally friendly fresh vegetables because of the strong and established reverse relationship between eating vegetables and the risk of many types of chronic and degenerative diseases such as cancer, cardiovascular and neurological diseases. Due to this growing consumer interest, the content of healthpromoting substances is becoming an essential consideration for producers of fruit and vegetables. Fresh fruits and vegetables are rich sources of bioactive substances with important health benefits, and these useful substances can be influenced by various important factors, including genotype selection and environmental conditions (light, temperature, humidity, CO_2) atmospheric). In contrast to the conventional agricultural system, hydroponics is based on the manipulation of nutrients, which, according to various authors, has made possible a strong accumulation of certain useful nutrients. However, questions are often asked about their safety. Considerable research has been done on conventional and hydroponic production, but few have compared the impact of the two on the nutritional quality of fresh vegetables. In this context, we discuss with this chapter with updated information on the differences between hydroponics and conventional production and the impact of hydroponics on the nutritional composition and the levels of bioactive compounds. We discuss their impact, their limitations, and their success.

The idea of not necessarily needing arable land to grow plants may seem far-fetched, but with the advancement of hydroponics, it is nowadays a reality. Hydroponics, a simple method that allows plants to grow with water and essential mineral nutrients, is quickly becoming a popular option. Hydroponics is essentially a branch of agriculture where you grow landless plants. Instead of the soil, you can use a nutrient solution prepared by dissolving the nutrients in the water. The nutrient solution gives your plants the nutrients they would otherwise get out of the ground. Etymologically "hydroponics" comes from the Greek words "hydro" - water and "bonus" - work. Hydroponics is a plant-growing technique that mainly uses water as a basis; or in other words, it is a bottomless cultivation process. In the absence of soil to provide nutrients, hydroponics uses methods such as the food film technique (NFT) to collect plant food. Hydroponics does not mean that your plants are completely at the mercy of the water. There are natural growing media that you can use instead of earth and tested hydroponic nutrients developed by companies that have years of proven success in making hydroponic nutritional formulas. Among other things, you can use hydroponics growing media such as prelate, gravel, sand, coconut instead of soil, depending on the crop you choose for hydroponics. As the population grows and the arable land becomes scarcer and more expensive, this revolutionary technology becomes more and more popular. Plants can be grown in greenhouses, multistory buildings, basements or roofs. Gardening on the roof using a hydroponic system is also common in large cities where the costs of delivery are the earth is very high. Hydroponics is an easy and practical technique to adopt, it becomes easier and easier to become an amateur cultivator. You grow more plants in the same area than you could with the help of soil-based cultivation techniques. It is an ecological technique that helps save water and you can even recycle it if you are aware of the consumption of this invaluable and limited resource. You can use hydroponic growing media such as prelate, gravel, sand, coconut and other materials instead of soil, depending on the crop you choose. What you get from hydroponics is much more than you would expect from soil culture and traditional farming techniques. The yield of hydroponics is much higher - almost 30 to 35% more. With the increasing food shortages in the world, hydroponics can be the solution to the food shortage. Because hydroponics takes up less space, it will not disrupt existing green cover by reducing the amount of forest that can be converted into agricultural areas. Hydroponics does not depend on the climate and is most effective when plants are grown indoors. You have several options for growing your hydroponic plant - from a simple grows room to a temperature-controlled greenhouse.

Chapter 1

General Hydroponics - Use Hydroponics For Better Yields

Growing wheatgrass with hydroponics

Hydroponics is a simple method for growing plants without soil. It saves garden space, is cheaper and is very affordable in many ways. The hydroponics method increases the yield, requires less space and is both profitable and ecological. Indoor gardening is possible with the help of hydroponics. You can have total control over the temperature, humidity, plant nutrition and the climate of your hydroponic garden. If you have a basic knowledge of gardening, you can successfully build your hydroponic garden! Wheatgrass is a nutritious plant that can offer you many health benefits. You no longer have to go to the market or fields and waste your time collecting wheatgrass that can be juicy or of good quality. With hydroponics, you can plant your healthy wheat garden. Hydroponics is the cleanest method of producing wheatgrass. With the right nutrients and water supply, you can successfully grow wheat in your hydroponic garden. You will be surprised by the rapid cultivation of wheatgrass using hydroponics! You can grow wheatgrass indoors with hydroponics at any time of the year and as often as you want. To build a simple and simple hydroponic garden with wheatgrass, all you have to do is follow the basic steps for hydroponics gardening:

- As with traditional gardening, you should start hydroponic wheatgrass gardening by buying seeds from a local dealer;
- Place the seeds evenly in the container so that they cover the entire floor of the container;
- Immerse the seeds in the water halfway. Note, do not completely cover the container with water;
- Now you can cover the drawer with the second drawer or another plastic cover because the seeds don't need light first, but

make sure you don't close the drawer because the seeds need air;

- Water your hydroponic wheatgrass daily with a spray bottle and as soon as you see that your plants have started sprouting, add water slowly enough as your plants grow. In addition to this simple, home-made cultivation method for wheatgrass, you can purchase the hydroponic grow set from your local hydroponic store. This wheat-growing set contains all the components you need to grow your hydroponic wheat effectively. Right away the small initial investment, you can have your tray with fresh and healthy wheatgrass. Be careful when choosing your hydroponic wheat kit because not all trays guarantee the freshness of good quality of hydroponic wheatgrass!

Hydroponic herb garden
Hydroponics is a method for growing plants in water; it is a method for growing plants without soil. In

addition to tomatoes and lettuce grown in hydroponics, important herbs such as basil, arugula, oregano, lemon balm, etc. can be grown using the hydroponics system. The nutritional requirements of hydroponic herbs can vary from plant to plant. It is possible to grow several hydroponic herbs in a single nutrient solution, but special attention must be paid to the prevention of hydroponic herbs against nutrient deficiencies. There are three main types of hydroponic herbs for different purposes; for example, there are herbs that can be used specifically for cooking (culinary herbs), there are medicinal herbs (home healing) and ornamental herbs. It can be grown in a single unit for a year without setting up the unit to grow the news again, as opposed to growing hydroponic fruit and vegetables where you need to clean the hydroponic unit after harvest to start over. You can build your hydroponic garden for cooking. Hydroponic herbal systems are automated and easy to use. Common and easy to grow kitchen herbs are basil, mint, oregano, and parsley, which improve the taste of your food. Herbal remedies are ginger root, kava-kava, violet, and gravel root. And the ornamental herbs used for decoration or presentation are sage, rosemary and chamomile. The three main types of simple hydroponic growth systems are the food film technique (NFT), the Ebb and Flow averages and the aerologic agents. It can easily be done anywhere, indoors or out, with a simple gardening method. For successful gardening, you have to understand the desired pH of the plant, the soil needs, water needs, possible pests, etc. Herbs grown in hydroponics appear to be healthier, tastier and fresher than traditionally grown herbs. These herbs are free from chemicals and fertilizers. Medicinal hydroponic herbs are simple and reliable. Hydroponic marijuana is an important ingredient in therapies to cure AIDS and cancer; it also works as a painkiller under certain circumstances. Hydroponics herbs have been used for decades for therapeutic programs. Another medicinal benefit of marijuana or weed is the treatment of glaucoma, a condition that causes vision loss. Growing hydroponic weeds is a wise choice because it helps to cure many diseases while sitting at home.

Medicinal gardening can easily be done at home and can be used immediately in tea and extracts

Hydroponic grow sets for the indoor gardener

Many people turn to the garden to reduce food costs for their families and to make contact with nature. However, if you live in an area where outdoor gardening is out of the question, such as an apartment building or a hostile environment that needs to be dry or cold for plants to thrive, it may be a bitter disappointment to want to do gardening, but without a real way to continue to go. This is when hydroponic culture sets can come in handy. Hydroponics packages help the novice gardener succeed with indoor hydroponic gardening, as they all contain materials you need to start this exciting hobby. Although hydroponics packages vary from manufacturer to manufacturer and depending on the type of hydroponics you want to do, some basic components are common. Because every type of plant needs water, food, and light to grow and thrive, you want to ensure that hydroponic systems reflect these needs. There are hydroponics lamps in kit form and it is an easy way to start building hydroponics systems. Hydroponics lamps can be LEDs or HID lamps, which orequire a digital ballast to function properly, as well as reflectors and possibly fans, depending on the number of lamps installed and the size of the room. Because hydroponics is a form of aquatic gardening where no soil is used, each of the hydroponics packages you are considering has a way to retain water or place water around the roots of the plants. However, the crown of the plants must be kept out of the water so that they do not rot, and this is achieved with hydroponic supplies such as nets or trays with holes in it so that only the roots are exposed in the water. Pumps and filters are used to move water and help supply oxygen, and pumps can also be used to raise and lower the water level depending on the system you choose to use. Lights and hardware are the usual components that are included in the hydroponic kits. A final piece that you need to ensure proper growth and production in your plants is food, which is called hydroponic nutrients in gardening.

Hydroponic nutrients contain all the macro and micronutrients that your plants need, and there are hundreds of formulations from which you can choose the formulations that best meet the needs of the specific plants that you want to grow in hydroponic packages.

Why hydroponics?

Hydroponic Gardens are compact and can be placed anywhere.

- They use and reuse water over and over and need at least extra water to function properly.

- They eliminate the need to control garden pests such as aphids, caterpillars, potato beetles, and fungi.

- They are very efficient growers for plants - plants grow very quickly in a hydroponics configuration.

- They are practical and most systems are easy to automate, so they require minimal interference from you. Every plant can grow (or start growing) in a hydroponic system, regardless of the time of year or the north or south position.

There are other reasons why hydroponics is preferable to a traditional garden, but there are also disadvantages. For example, many people associate hydroponic gardening with the growth of certain illegal plants that are often used as controlled substances. It seems that every week a large house in a nice neighborhood is destroyed by the police with hundreds of compact fluorescent lamps, water sprays, containers, dust, nutrients, and plants removed. However, like everything, a small percentage of people can ruin something good for everyone. In reality, the main benefits of hydroponics gardening are to give people who would otherwise be unable to grow plants the opportunity to grow plants. It is very common for passionate gardeners to start their delicate young plants in a hydroponics configuration and then transfer these plants to their gardens after the soil has thawed. Orchid growers, in particular, seem to be inclined towards hydroponic cultivation systems. The obsession that many people have with orchids is intense. This obsession, combined with the frustration of not being able to meet the demanding needs of the orchid in the unchanged backyard of a person, encourages many to try to grow in greenhouses or hydroponic facilities. Moreover, hydroponics technology is everywhere. Light timers are used in many applications to save energy, just as they are used in hydroponics to time the light cycle of plants. Compact fluorescent lamps, metal halide, T5 and other types of intense lighting used in hydroponics are also used in aquarium systems that strive to meet the demanding needs of freshwater plants or delicate corals and anemones. Water drop systems are regularly used in greenhouses and large-scale agriculture, but also gardening and landscaping. Plant nutrients have been developing for quite some time - as long as people are trying to grow non-native plants in partially impoverished soils. The pH meters are used in scientific applications and still in all forms of gardening. We would not know where the acidic soils would grow the grapes if we did not use a pH tester, apart from costly falls and getting up. Hydroponics grew out of a combination of need and desire. We want fresh tomatoes, we want fresh basil, and we need a place to grow them because we don't all live on farms anymore. The more we hear about plants covered with wax and pesticides, the more we worry about these substances that end up in our children and ourselves, and we want a way to be sure of our food sources. Although it is impossible to think that we can go from buying our food in the store to growing everyone in our apartments, it is good to know that we can supplement some of our products in this way. Special sauces, for example, or your herb garden for fresh coriander, basil and oregano are a tempting reason to switch to hydroponics. For pure and hard natural gardens, hydroponics may not be your cup of tea. If you use plants from your region, simply sow your seeds and let nature take its course. However, for many in northern climates, waiting for spring is too far away. These people appreciate the plant life that technology can bring to their homes. Something to keep in mind: Before this writer knew what hydroponics was, she bought "tomatoes aged in vines and grown in hydroponics" from the local supermarket because of their color, texture and superior taste. They were constantly bright red, juicy and free of stains. They were always smaller than the so-called "stew pot tomatoes", but the larger, lightercolored tomatoes had a less rich taste. The balance of nutrients, light, and water, combined with the reduced need of the plant to fight infections, insects and fungi, produces a much healthier plant specimen than would otherwise be possible.

Forget organic - go hydroponics!

People pay more for organic products, but did you know that there is an even cleaner way to grow all your fruit and vegetables at home, without paying a penny in the supermarket? Market leader, Great Stuff Hydroponics, wants to explain how this is possible. Known as hydroponics, the science of growing plants without using soil is becoming the next big thing among environmentally friendly consumers with green fingers. Instead of extracting nutrients from the soil, plant roots are directly exposed to nutrient solutions, giving them balanced nutrition in a controlled indoor environment. This method can be used to grow plants all over the world in every season.

The soil cannot contaminate the edible parts of the plant, and therefore hydroponically grown plants are not a risk for soil diseases and are much less susceptible to pests. As a result, plants are naturally healthier than their soil counterparts (geoponics). Many commercially grown hydroponic plants do not require pesticides and are certified organic. Hydroponics of plants also has many environmental benefits. Hydroponics the method uses only about 1/20th of the water used for irrigation on farms to produce the same amount of food. Normally the "drain" of farms ends up in the water surface. Hydroponic growth therefore considerably reduces the effects of large-scale agriculture on the water level, with the added advantage that the water used and its effects on the surrounding land can be accurately measured. Hydroponic plants are already commercially grown on a large scale in Israel, Nicaragua and the United States, where people can grow fresh produce with limited water supply in arid landscapes. Going to buy or grow hydroponics fruits and vegetables also has certain benefits for the consumer; there is a shorter delay between picking and packing the plant, which means that it stays fresh longer. Moreover, because hydroponic plants have better access to the sun and better nutrition, the products can be healthier and tastier. Steven Parker, director of Great Stuff Hydroponics, says: "Growing hydroponic plants is something anyone can do at home with one of the Great Stuff Hydroponic kits, for beginners or advanced growers. Because of the methods used you can get all your favorite vegetables and growing fruit. Out of season home. "

How to mix hydroponic nutrients

Plants that are traditionally grown in the soil can extract essential nutrients from the soil, but if you grow with a hydroponic system, it is up to you to ensure that everything your plants need is in the nutrient solution. You can choose ready-made hydroponic nutrients to concentrate and simply add a certain amount of water. It is also a good alternative to make a simple and inexpensive hydroponic nutritional solution yourself with the help of basic ingredients.

This is how:

1. Pour just enough water into a tank, tub, bucket or another container to fill the tank with nutrients for your hydroponic system. Be sure to measure the number of gallons.

2. Check the pH value of the water that you are going to use in your nutrient mix, using a pH test kit for hydroponics systems. You can buy this kit from hydroponics stores and suppliers. The pH must be between 5.0 and 6.0. If the level is outside this range, use the chemicals in your kits to adjust the pH level down or up until it is within this range.

3. Measure two teaspoons for every gallon of a complete dry water-soluble fertilizer. Use a fertilizer with micronutrients such as magnesium, sulfur, potassium, nitrogen, phosphorus, and calcium. Also make sure it contains essential micronutrients such as boron,

zinc, chlorine, cobalt, manganese, iron, copper, and molybdenum. Then add this fertilizer to the water.

4. Add one teaspoon of Epsom salt for every liter of water.

5. Mix all dry ingredients in water until all crystals and powder dissolve in the well.

6. Remove and replace your nutrient solution every one to two weeks to ensure that the plants have the nutrients they need continuously.

Advice

If your tank contains a lot of water in your hydroponics system, mix one or two extra batches of hydroponics. Never overfill the container, otherwise the hydroponic nutrients spill by mixing. Use the solution immediately after mixing, as it may lose some strength when you store it for use.

Warnings

If the water level falls between changes due to absorption or evaporation, only use normal water to replace what has been lost. Adding a new batch of nutrient solutions to the old one can cause an imbalance and salts that can damage the plants can accumulate. This type of fertilizer is best used in ebb and flow hydroponics systems, hydroponics raft configurations, and other hydroponics systems that do not tend to clog. Hydroponic systems such as geoponics or drip hydroponics can become clogged when solids reach the nozzles.

Hydroponic garden backyard vs. Hydroponic greenhouse

The growth of plants in the courtyard of your hydroponics may not seem ideal in the use of Hydroponic greenhouse. A hydroponic greenhouse offers better lighting and irrigation on the configuration of the system. Not many people will support the greenhouse concept if they are used to the hydroponic garden system. You need sufficient space for the installation of irrigation systems and lighting systems that are needed for the hydroponic gardens. Where is space available in this fast-paced world full of houses and skyscrapers? But if you have a hydroponic greenhouse, you can place these systems much easier and also in a smaller space. Lighting and other arrangements are supplied with the greenhouse, so you don't have to worry about those factors. Most plants that do well under hydroponic conditions are carefully examined. Gravel is usually seen as a means to support the root user, and a balanced mix of all nutrients flows cultures regularly in liquid form. This method is called a "subculture of irrigation". In a large, perfect hydroponic greenhouse, once the plants have been planted, the entire work is supported by automation. Sensors in the gravel determine when the plants need more solutions, based on which they control the pumps accordingly. The biggest advantage of using hydroponics in the garden is light. To be successful, the plants grown in hydroponics need a lot of light. But don't forget that too much light allows algae to thrive, and they don't want that. In a hydroponics greenhouse, sunlight is filtered and spread over time. You can also specify or control the number and angle of light by using colors and shutters. Another advantage is that you need less energy because you do not continue to grow lightly. You will also find that procedures for supplying plant nutrition are easier to install and maintain if you have a hydroponic greenhouse. This is of course very important for the health of plants in hydroponics. If the plants do not grow in the soil, the pH is very different. You will see large fluctuations in acidity and alkalinity because it is water-based. A hydroponics configuration in a greenhouse is simple; setting an automatic pH control keeps checking the figures. And you don't have to worry about how your plants will stay warm in the winter. A good greenhouse has an acceptable temperature, even in cold weather without heat. This is especially useful if you live in an area with a lower temperature but lots of sunshine. Fans and vents can also be installed to control the temperature in your greenhouse. Remember that it is important to control the temperature of plants in hydroponic gardening. You can build your hydroponic greenhouse or buy it ready. Yes! You can get it in different sizes and styles. Many models also take into account the expansion of the garden in the future. It may be time for you to have a hydroponic greenhouse and have these favorite fruits or vegetable gardens.

Chapter 2

Aero Hydroponics

Aero hydroponics is a more complicated type of hydroponics where oxygen is introduced into the nutrient solution that constantly occupies the roots of the plant. The growing media that can be used are rock wool, vine tongs, net pots or other means to support plants to expose their roots to the air. By exposing the roots to air, they can absorb nutrients evenly and quickly. This promotes larger crops and faster development. Plants that can be used in an aero-hydroponic system are melons, cucumbers, strawberries, and many others. Aero hydroponics can be a bit more sensitive than other types of hydroponics systems. That said, aerodynamics can also be a more efficient way to grow organic crops. Even if aero-hydroponics systems must have more complex equipment than other methods, the use of this method has many advantages. **How aero-hydroponics works**

Of all the different available hydroponics methods, the aero hydro pony is the most avant-garde.

Gardeners who use this system can help their plants reach their full potential because of the increased amount of dissolved oxygen absorbed by the roots. The extra oxygen helps plants to grow better. Oxygen is introduced into the edge of the roots when the nutrient solution is sprayed into the air, allowing the oxygen to mix with the solution and eventually be absorbed by the roots. This system is profitable because after the initial investment there is practically no waste in disposable items such as culture media.

Construction of the aero-hydroponics system

To build an aerodynamic system, you can use different components that can be used in different ways in different designs. In every design, the idea is that plants should be supported in a way that allows the roots to hang. The spray of the nutrient solution is located under the roots. There must be sufficient space to be able to mix a good mix of air and solution. You can design your system or purchase a pre-made system. A system that you can configure at home is the Aeroflot system. The most important components in this system are a pump, a tank and individual culture containers in a support structure. This system is available in different sizes, depending on your needs. The growing containers provide the support that plants need, while oxygen, air, and solution can reach the roots. Maintenance of this system is fairly easy. The nutrient solution must be changed every two weeks, the conductivity or amount of total dissolved salts must be kept at 800-1200 ppm and the pH must be kept at around 5.5 to 6.5. The pH remains fairly stable in this system because the culture medium is not used. The only time the pH is adjusted is when you mix a new batch of nutrient solution. Various obstacles prevented farmers from taking advantage of the benefits of an aero-hydroponic system, such as the initial costs for building a system and problems with permits. After discovering the efficiency of aero-hydroponics systems, some producers are already taking on the challenge of investing in these systems. If this hydroponic method is used by commercial

agriculture, it will only continue to evolve

Why does the environment benefit from hydroponics?

Global warming has become a major problem in the 21st century, whether you are an average citizen or a government leader. Scientists are always looking for better ways to reduce carbon dioxide emissions and protect the environment. Research suggests that the best way for a country to reduce toxic greenhouse gases is to control how food is produced and delivered. Fruits and vegetables grown in hydroponics offer many possibilities, not only to produce larger and tastier vegetables but also to protect the environment. Let's look at the most important ways in which hydroponics could be the way to become "green" in the future.

As you already know, hydroponics uses less land. Recent studies have shown that about 10 million hectares of arable land are lost every year. For centuries, farmers have increasingly squeezed the amount of land that can be used for traditional soil cultivation; hydroponics can prove to be the solution.

Hydroponic growth gives you complete control over yields and produces the same amount of vegetables in just 1/5 of the space. Hydroponics can grow vegetables anywhere - this is the most important factor because it reduces the distance that food may have to travel to reach its destination. When a vegetable is out of season in one part of the world, the season is in another part. These vegetables are therefore often produced and shipped to areas where they are not in season, where scarcity can push up prices. To meet the ever-increasing demand for food, transporting food requires a lot of fossil fuel due to theft. With hydroponics, you can grow almost every vegetable in every season in every part of the world, so that they can be grown closer to their point of sale and use less gas. They usually taste better too, because of the shorter distance they have to travel means that they can be picked when they are ripe.

Hydroponics uses less water; when watering a typical ground garden, much of the water used is lost to the ground, which means that much more water must be used. Water is recycled in a hydroponic garden. This puts much less stress on the increasingly tense water supply. It causes less land erosion - traditional agriculture requires plowing the land, which can contribute to land erosion. Hydroponic gardening does not use any soil and therefore there are no significant changes to the soil, this problem can be completely avoided. Pesticides that are often needed to prevent insects from destroying traditional crops. This means less poison on plants, in rivers and, more importantly, on the food we eat. All these factors, together with the improved taste that can result from this culture style, have made hydroponics the choice of many large-scale greenhouses. Up to 90% of British Columbia greenhouses use hydroponics. As the benefits of hydroponics become clearer over time, more greenhouses will follow.

Hydroponics: the future of agriculture

Hydroponics is the method to grow almost any plant without burying it in the soil. A few centuries ago, botanists realized that plants absorb nutrients through the water that penetrates the soil around their roots.

The soil only functions as a food reservoir and as an environment in which the plant can stabilize. If the water supplied to a plant already contains the necessary organic matter and the plant is protected or suspended by another method or material, the soil becomes useless. This discovery aroused botanists and interested parties involved in agriculture, but it did not cause an immediate revolution in agriculture. In the 20th century, when people were worried about the presence of pesticides and other toxins in crops that were grown on a large scale, the interest in hydroponics suddenly increased. Crops produced with hydroponics methods do not require pesticides and do not pose a threat to humans.

How plants grow hydroponically from seeds

Many hydroponics growers prefer to grow hydroponics plants from seedlings or cuttings from another plant - often from a plant that is grown in the soil. Although you can get away with it, this introduces a multitude of problems that do not exist when growing from seeds. The advantage of hydroponics is that you can produce higher yields than plants grown in the soil and that your plants do not suffer from the same pests and soil diseases as plants grown in the soil. The seeds do not contain the pests and diseases that are present in the seedlings. If you buy seedlings from a nursery where diseases and pests are common, you run the risk of infecting your hydroponic garden and ruining your plants. Aphids are common in daycare centers and are difficult to recognize. When buying a seedling, the roots are rinsed to remove the soil before they are transferred to a hydroponic solution. Some plants find it difficult to transplant from the soil into a hydroponic environment.

If you want to get the satisfaction that comes from growing seeds and fully through your efforts, you need the following kit:

- Groan Rockwool plugs
- Hydroponic plateau
- Heating mat
- Cultivate light or natural light

- Sowing solution

Growing small seeds in granular hydroponics will simply cause the small seeds to fall through the cracks when exposed to a hydroponics solution. Starting plugs must be made of inorganic materials, have a diameter of approximately 2 or 3 inches and must be shallow enough so that the seeds are never far from the nutrient solution and therefore kept moist. Groan Rockwool plugs are ideal for this purpose. Simply use a pencil to make different holes in each starting plug. For most plants, 2 seeds per cube should be sufficient, for herbs 4 to 6 seeds per cube are more suitable. Place each of the starter plugs in a slot in the hydroponic dish to hold them in place. Add the hydroponic solution in this drawer. Place a clear plastic dome cover on the drawer. You can buy a hydroponic fruit dome that is specially designed for seedlings. Some even you can adjust the humidity with adjustable ventilation openings. The container must retain moisture and heat the air around the plants. It must also be transparent because seedlings need a lot of light to grow. A seedling heating mat can be placed under the pan to ensure that the seedlings are kept warm. A temperature between 70 and 80 degrees Fahrenheit is ideal. Water once or twice a week, depending on how quickly the tank dries. You must add a seed solution in the container and not directly on top of the plant. The hydroponic solution must be approximately 5.5 and have the correct concentration. It must also contain the necessary macro and micronutrients found in most hydroponic nutritional solutions. The seeds should start to germinate within a few days and the plants should be a few centimeters long within 1 to 3 weeks.

The roots must also be visible from the outside of the starting plug. You have to leave the strongest seedlings in a single cap and at the same time remove the least healthy ones. When the roots begin to appear through the plugs, it is time to transfer the plants to a larger unit. Do not remove the roots from the starter plug, but place the plugin in the hydroponic unit. You must ensure that the seedlings are kept moist and that the roots have access to the nutritious water solution. Moreover, the growing plant must be exposed to a lot of light as it ages.

Chapter 3

The Secrets Of Master Hydroponics Producers

Nutrients: the perfect mix Foods that your plant cannot do without all plants need nutrients in the form of macronutrients and micronutrients to grow well and achieve the ideal yield. The same applies to hydroponics gardening. The first group consists mainly of nitrogen, phosphorus and potassium, and secondary calcium, magnesium, and sulfur. Some of the micronutrients that plants need are boron, manganese, copper, zinc, chloride, iron and molybdenum. When growing your favorite plant, it is necessary to use the perfect nutrient mixes that vary depending on the specific growth phases in which they are located, otherwise, your investment will go into its disposal. These are the foods that your favorite plant needs to survive, to give the fruit you want in terms of quantity and quality, and to grow healthily enough to reproduce.

Nitrogen: plants need to produce the proteins and enzymes used in photosynthesis and also to activate the metabolic processes involved. The healthy and correct dosage of this nutrient ensures the quality of the leaves of your fruit and the rapid production of seeds. Phosphorus: it is primarily involved in the formation of oils and starches in plants. If necessary, it helps to convert the sun into chemical energy, giving your plant greater tolerance for stress and good maturation.

Potassium: it helps in the production of proteins and guarantees plants better resistance to diseases.

Calcium: it makes the cell walls of plants stronger and gives them greater resistance.

Magnesium: it is essential for photosynthesis because it is an important part of chlorophyll.

Sulfur: this nutrient improves plant growth and their resistance to cold.

Boron: it is an essential element in the production of seeds and fruits from plants.

Copper: it is an important ingredient in the reproductive processes of plants.

Zinc: this regulates plant growth. It produces axing, which is an essential growth hormone. Zinc is also essential for the root development of the plant and the formation of starch.

Iron: an ingredient in making chlorophyll. A shortage of plant iron can be minimized by choosing a soil that is suitable for the growing conditions of the plant.

Molybdenum: it helps with the use of nitrogen. This important nutrient is important in the formation of pollen.

Manganese: helps with the breakdown of nitrogen and carbohydrates.

Magic mixing ratios that your favorite plants love Just like children, your favorite plants in your hydroponic garden need the right nutrition to become productive and healthy. Too many and too few nutrients cause problems that cause mental anxiety and financial setbacks. You must consider their growth phases before you give them a mixture, which is as follows.

The vegetative phase refers to this short moment when the plant starts photosynthesis. This also refers to the growing period when it develops its height, the thickness of the stems, potential bud locations and side branches. The flowering phase or fruit phase, which you will find very satisfactory, is the period in which your plants show their genus and bear flowers.

NPK 2: 1: 1 ratio

During the vegetative or growth phase of your hydroponic gardening, your plants must receive a 2: 1: 1 portion of nitrogen (N), phosphorus (P) and potassium (K). Here are some tips on suitable proportions that can be used during the vegetative phase:

A ratio of 20:10:10. This would mean that 20% of the mixture should be nitrogen, 10% phosphorus, 10% potassium and the remaining 60% should be composed of secondary macronutrients and micronutrients. A ratio of 30:15:15. This would require 30% of the nitrogen, 15% phosphorus and 15% potassium mixture. The remaining 20% consists of secondary macronutrients and micronutrients. These mixing ratios give your plants more resources during photosynthesis and result in better quality leaves and seeds.

The mix of flowers

When your favorite plants start flowering, adjust the ratio to 1: 2: 2 nitrogen, phosphorus, and potassium. The mixture must contain more phosphorus and potassium than nitrogen. If you use the 20: 10: 10 ratio during the growth phase, use the 10: 20: 20 ratio during the flowering phase. And if you use the 30: 15: 15 ratio during the vegetative period, you must use the 15: 30: 30 ratio during the flowering period. With these ratios, your plants become stronger and they tolerate greater stress tolerance. Moreover, it is even suggested that you can stop feeding your plants with nitrogen during the flowering phase of your hydroponic horticulture project and you can concentrate on phosphorus, potassium, magnesium, and sulfur. Eating too much could kill people.

10 friendly tips about formulation and diet

There are two ways to get the magic mix and the right proportions. You buy pre-formulated nutrients or you only formulate them. In the first option, you only need to combine a standard amount that is prescribed by the manufacturers of the concentrate with water. However, the second option is the most cost-effective and efficient because your mixes are based on what your plants would need. Whatever you choose, there are considerations that you should not forget, such as the pH level or the acid content of the formula, because the ability of the roots to absorb nutrients depends on it. Here are some friendly tips that you can view and consider: Keep the pH value of your formulas in the best range for your favorite plants, which is 5.8 to 6.5. A pH level of 1 is acidic, 7 neutral and 14 basics. You can measure the pH level with a chemical test kit to be refilled when the materials are consumed or with electronic methods such as pens with LCD monitors immersed in the solution. Adjust the pH level if necessary. This can be done with distilled vinegar. A perfect mix or balance between phosphoric acid, nitric acid, and sulfuric acid is important, especially because they maximize the potential benefits that your plants can derive from nutrients such as phosphorus, nitrogen, and sulfur. You can use potassium Hydroxide and sodium hydroxides to increase the basic PHS You can also use soft drinks as a balancing agent. Use alternative hydroponics systems to feed plants with nutrients other than those already in use. The most commonly used systems are geoponics, continuous solution culture, static solution culture, flooding and drainage sub-irrigation, passive sub-irrigation, top irrigation, irrigation by ultrasound and culture in deep water. Alternative feeding systems include the use of pre-processed coconut fibers. They contain less potassium and sodium and are very rich in magnesium and calcium, both of which are very useful for increasing or improving the growth of your plants. Replace the nutrient solution every two weeks. Remove the old solution from the tank and clean the equipment with hot water to kill unwanted bacteria that have collected. Recycle the old solution. Instead of throwing it away, use it to water the plants. Maintain the level of the water reservoir. Make sure you check it daily, as the water evaporates faster on hot days. Do not overdo the feeding. Too many nutrients can kill your beloved plants and cause large losses. Dissolve the powder solution before placing it in the tank water. If you use concentrated liquids, mix them better before placing them directly in the water. Stop feeding your plant nutrients at least seven days before harvesting. However, continue with the water supply. Oxygen on your water. You can age tap water for three days by placing it in a container.

Ventilation: heat management Due to the sensitivity of the plants to climate change, you have to manage the heat well in your hydroponic garden. Some countries only have two seasons: wet and dry; and one of them is Australia. Dry seasons usually last six months when the temperature is lower. During the wet seasons, which usually also last six months, there is too much rain and the temperature is high due to the increase in humidity. For hydroponics producers like you, these weather changes can present many challenges, because when using artificial light the natural temperature is increased by the heat emitted by artificial light. The more power you use, the more heat is generated. Too much heat can kill your favorite plants before they even grow or bloom.

What you can do

Various things can be done to control the heat - to raise or lower it. You have to learn to deal with heat because it can be too low or too high. If it is too low, your plants will die from cold; and with that too low, their leaves will curl and eventually die. These are simple things you can do: Use air conditioners or ventilation systems to control the airflow and therefore the temperature of your hydroponic room. If air conditioners are too expensive for you in terms of electricity consumption, make a ventilation system. The most common ventilation systems are those that circulate warm air from the ceiling of your plant room to another room. Other ventilation systems are installed to extract air through the chimney, walls or even roofs. You can use simple equipment, such as bathroom fans, like a drain. Check the humidity and temperature in your hydroponic growing area using a thermometer. Create a system that can remove heat in five minutes and twenty-five-minute cycles when the artificial light is on. You need a timer and a fan of this type of system. Set up a system based on a thermostat. It will automatically switch on a fan or air conditioner when a specific temperature or heat level is reached and switch off the cooling equipment when the level drops by at least 4 degrees Celsius. For internal air movement, oscillating fans will succeed. It will facilitate the circulation of carbon dioxide and at the same time reduce installation humidity in the garden. This is necessary to reduce the incidence of plant diseases caused by fungi and to absorb moisture in the room. To prevent temperature drops, which usually occur during the night or when your artificial lighting is switched off, you must install a propane heating set that is coordinated with a thermostat or timer. If you decide to use a thermostat, set it to detect a temperature drop below 20 degrees Celsius and to switch the heating on and off as soon as the heating level is 30 degrees Celsius. Besides, this system provides your plants with more carbon dioxide sources, an essential part of photosynthesis.

Hydroponic supplies - Basic information for hydroponics producers

Which hydroponic supplies do you need to get started? Let's take a look at some basic concepts of hydroponics to help you succeed in your business. Hydroponics is a type of indoor garden that uses hydroponic nutrients instead of the soil. This nutrient solution offers everything plants need to grow healthily. There are different basic types of hydroponic supplies that you need if you want to grow hydroponic plants. Of course, not everyone needs the same hydroponic supplies - what you buy depends on the type of system you want to use. Most systems require a tank or large tank, an aerator and a pump to move the solution and keep it welloxygenated, and a method to keep the plants above the solution, such as a container or a net. The roots must be able to dissolve without drowning the plant. Lighting is also a major concern. When buying hydroponic supplies, pay attention to your lighting options. If you grow a large number of plants or plants that usually need a lot of sunshine, you may need to buy fairly strong lights. Remember - the goal is to imitate sunlight. Some growers mainly opt for lighting in the blue and green spectra to stimulate faster growth, especially in seedlings. However, these are not the only lights in the section on hydroponics supplies. You also need lights in the red spectrum. These simulate late-summer lighting and help to promote the fruiting and flowering of adult plants. Consider using reflectors to increase light coverage.

Manage the energy flow with the help of digital ballasts, which ensure that your lighting remains uniform. Of course, some lights work quite warm. Choose fans from your hydroponic supply retailer to cool them and prevent your plants from burning or wilting. The culture medium is also important. You can purchase commercial support or make your mix from a set of chemicals. Add a cloner and you have a full range of hydroponic supplies. It takes a small investment to get started, but you will be glad that you did if you grow your hydroponic plants indoors! Take the time to assess the available space and budget, determine what you want to develop and discover which suppliers are available to you. Make a list before you go shopping and compare prices before you buy. You will get a lot, and the ability to grow plants like you've never had before. Choose the right hydroponic supplies to get the best results from your growing efforts. You will not regret it.

Hydroponic lights

Hydroponics - agriculture using hydroponic tents and hydroponic lamps. Hydroponics, otherwise known as water cultivation, is a technique in which varieties of plants are grown in hydroponic tents and hydroponic lamps without soil to provide plants with nutrients. Instead of using the soil as an agent to provide nutrients to plants, water mixed with minerals and nutrients is used as an agent to provide all of the nutrients and minerals to the plant needs.

Hydroponics has made great strides, especially in the last century due to the larger crops that have been obtained by growing plants under hydroponic tents and hydroponic lights, whatever the seasons and weather situation. However, the first results published in the early 1900s showed that the yield of the plant grown under hydroponic tents and hydroponics lamps is not at all superior to the yield of plants grown on the ground. When the whole world thought hydroponics was just a fake, there was a breakthrough. Wake Island, an island in the North Pacific, was the place where hydroponics was a real success, you could say. The island had little land to grow plants and the islanders could get a good harvest by growing the plants using hydroponics techniques. One of the main reasons why part of the population still believes that hydroponics will soon be hugely successful is that the farmer knows the exact amount of water he needs to grow a plant, as opposed to planting in a soil where he has little knowledge of the amount of water he needs to feed there. Because the roots of plants are exposed to a constant supply of oxygen as a result of the hydroponic solution, the plant is generally much healthier. And there is a big possibility that you can open all your gardening and farming indoors because the light needed for the plants is provided by hydroponic lamps and the protection of the plants with hydroponic tents. Moreover, total agriculture costs less than half of what you spend on real agriculture. A major advantage that you have to grow your plants in hydroponic tents under hydroponic light is that you can move the tent with minimal effort and even the water used to grow the plant can be recycled. Everything has its disadvantages, hydroponics too. Even the maintenance costs are very low compared to real agriculture, the starting costs, including the purchase of hydroponic tents and hydroponic lamps, are slightly higher. The person doing hydroponics must have a good knowledge of the solutions to be used and the conditions of the plant to ensure a successful harvest. But most hydroponics farmers say that once you get there, hydroponics farming is nothing but pure joy

Installation of a thermo-hygrometer

You can switch it on for 24 hours or more. This allows you to accurately monitor the humidity and temperature.

Lighting: fluorescent and HPS

Light is needed for your favorite plant, even in your hydroponics for photosynthesis and as indicators of time and seasons. With hydroponics lighting systems you can determine how long and how long plants are exposed to light to normalize photosynthesis cycles. With them, you can also simulate the seasons to encourage them. Bloom and extend the growing season so that you can enjoy your favorite plants and fruit all year round. Imagine that your plants continue to grow and bloom even in winter. When fats provide calories for humans, plants get them from light. With artificial light, your favorite plant can reach a height of six feet in three or four months.

Large artificial lighting systems

Your favorite hydroponic plant will certainly come into its own and offer you the best possible quality and quantity thanks to the following artificial lighting systems:

Fluorescent substances and LEDs (or light-emitting diodes) are best used at the stage when your plant seedlings begin to grow.

Metal halide (or MH) and high-pressure sodium systems (HPS) would be best for the flowering phase.

Fluorescent bulbs explained more

Fluorescent bulbs are ideal for seedlings and because of the low intensity they have to be placed closer to the plants. They must be hung at least eight to fifteen centimeters from the plants. They have the following benefits:

- Improved health and resistance of seedlings or cuttings
- Superior root growth and quality
- Maximize the response of plants in terms of photosynthesis
- Disclosure of metal halide spheres

They provide your hydroponics garden with abundant blue and green spectral light, essential for plant growth. This allows you to be sure that the growth of the leaves of your plant is maximized and that they become robust or compact. In comparison with fluorescent lamps and incandescent lamps, they are better for the flowering phase because their brightness is 125 lumens, which is quite large compared to the 18 lumens of incandescent lamps and 39 lumens of fluorescent lamps. They are both effective and efficient during the vegetative and flowering stages.

HPS lamps at their best

High-pressure sodium balls are considered to be the best for improving the budding and flowering processes of your favorite plants, as they emit light from the red and yellow spectrum. In other words, these are luminous lamps that mimic natural light. Most users prefer it during the flowering of their hydroponic garden.

Basic lighting tips that you need to practice

Whatever your favorite system is for your hydroponic garden, make sure you do the following to maximize the health, growth, and reproduction of your plants:

- Keep the young plant (s) continuously exposed to light for two months. Relieves them in the growth phase twenty-two hours a day; and if they bloom, keep them lit up for up to twelve hours a day. Keep the light close to the plants, but never let them touch the leaves. When the edges of their leaves curl, it means that they are overheated.

- During the growth phase, use light bulbs that emit blue or red bands from the spectrum. Metal halide lamps give blue light and fluorescent red light.

- The minimum exposure to light is twenty watts per foot. You can go much higher, but not too high, otherwise, your plants can roast and not too low because they can sag.

- Mount the lamps on the roof for more flexibility. As the plants grow, you can lift the bulbs higher.

- Use reflectors to ensure uniform lighting between all your plants. Those who don't get enough light because the others would become deformed, bigger and thinner.

- Plan and design a daily lighting cycle. If you don't, your plants will grow poorly. And if you wake them up when they are already used to the dark times of the day, they will be traumatized and can get sick.

- Paint your walls, roofs and even your floors with white to provide lighter reflectivity in your room. Brighten up the days of your favorites and make sure they feel loved and cared for.

Cloning: increase the success rate of your hydroponic gardening

Cloning simply means taking a cutting from your growing plant and placing it in a separate pot or container with other cuttings. Make sure that the clone you choose comes from female plants. When properly cared for, they become mature plants that are exact copies of the original or original plants. It is a method that would certainly help you to control the quality of your plants, seeds, and fruits. Clones grow faster than seeds, so you use time more efficiently.

Chapter 4

The Perpetual Harvest: Sea Of Green Techniques

These techniques involve the harvesting of batches of small plants that mature early. They refer to that method in hydroponic gardening where smaller plants are grown over shorter periods instead of growing a few big plants over a long time. With hydroponics where the environment is controlled from lighting to ventilation, it is possible to start one batch at an earlier time, and as they mature, another batch is started. This method results in a year-round growing and harvesting cycle. Another way of doing this is by starting all the plants together and creating a green canopy where you let your plant be harvested more times than once. Taller plants will be harvested from the top first without uprooting them. As the plant grows some more, the earlier lower level becomes the top that is ready for harvest.

Nadia Joy Adore is a work-at-home mother of two lovely daughters. She has been doing freelance work for more than three years now, catering to more than twenty clients from across the globe. When she's not writing or editing, she keeps herself busy playing or shopping with her two angels.

Hydroponics and quality of vegetable products

Hydroponics production is the method for growing plants in soilless (i.e. soilless) conditions with nutrients, water and an inert medium (including gravel, sand, and prelate).

From a plant-scientific perspective, there is no difference between above-ground plants and plants grown in the soil, because in both systems nutrients must first be dissolved in water plants can absorb them. The differences lie in the way nutrients are available for plants. In hydroponics, the nutrients are dissolved in the water and the solution enters the roots of the plants, which absorb water with minerals to different parts of the plant. In soil-based production, the elements adhere to soil particles and transfer to the soil solution, where they are absorbed by plant roots. There are different types of hydroponics, depending on how they are characterized. A criterion is to classify closed or open hydroponics systems. Hydroponics systems that do not use culture media are generally referred to as closed systems, whereas hydroponics systems with culture media can be closed or opened in a container, depending on whether the nutrient solution is recycled (closed) or with each irrigation cycle (open). In closed systems, nutrient concentrations are constantly recycled, controlled and adjusted, while in open systems the nutrient solution is discarded (but stored) after every feeding cycle. Another approach to classifying hydroponics systems is to classify them according to the movement of the nutrient solution: active or passive. Active means that the nutrient solution is displaced, usually by a pump, and is passively dependent on a wick or anchor of the culture medium. Others characterize hydroponics with criteria for recovery or non-recovery. Recovery occurs when the nutrient solution is re-introduced into the system, while non-recovery means that the nutrient solution is applied to the culture medium and then disappears. Although there is a wide range of criteria, there are three basic elements for plants: water/moisture, nutrients and oxygen. All these different types of hydroponics must offer these three basic things that are important for the successful production of plants. Despite this diversity, the criteria most commonly used by producers, farmers, private companies and researchers classify hydroponics systems in six different types: nutrient film technology (NFT), wicking system, ebb and flood (flood and drainage), aquaculture, the drip system, and the aerologic system.

Description of the hydroponic system

Geoponics this is the most advanced and high-tech method where plants are hung on special paths. The nutrients are sprayed directly onto the roots every few minutes, creating a light layer of nutrients. This system requires regular monitoring of the pumps to prevent malfunctions. Culture in deep water (DWC) In a DWC system, a tank is used to contain the nutrient solution. The roots of the plants are suspended from the nutrient solution to obtain a constant supply of water, oxygen, and nutrients. In this system, an air pump is used to supply the water with oxygen so that the roots cannot drown. Drip system in this system the nutrient solution is set aside in a tank and the plants are grown separately in a bottomless environment. Drip systems release nutrients very slowly through nozzles, and additional solutions can be collected and recycled, or even disposed of. With this system, it is possible to grow several types of plants at the same time. The ebb and flow are also called "flooding and drainage", the least used system in hydroponics. This system uses a breeding tank and a tank filled with a nutrient solution. A pump periodically floods the culture container with a nutrient solution, which then flows slowly. In this system, plants are normally grown in environments such as rock wool or gravel, but if they require a significant amount of moisture, this is replaced with vermiculite or coconut fiber due to their large capacity for retaining excessive moisture between floods. Nutrient Film (NFT) Technique Like geoponics, the Nutrient Film (NFT) technique is the most popular hydroponics system. With this method, a nutrient solution is continuously pumped through the channels in which the plants are placed. When the power solutions reach the end of the channel, they return to the beginning of the system. This makes it a recirculation system, but unlike DWC, the roots of the plant are not completely submerged, which is the main reason for calling this method NFT. Wick system this is the simplest and easiest hydroponics method. It is a completely passive system, which means that nutrients are stored in a tank and introduced into the root system through capillary action. With this system, we can find different growing media such as prelate, vermiculite, coconut fiber, and other formulations. The wick system is easy and inexpensive to install and maintain. The main disadvantage of this system is the poor oxygenation of the plant roots and a large amount of nutrient solution that is needed to effectively reach the plant root system.

Bioactive compounds

According to Biesalski et al, it is generally accepted that bioactive compounds can be defined as essential and non-essential compounds that are present in nature in the context of the food chain and have a positive effect on human health. Bioactive compounds consist of chemicals that occur in small quantities in plants (leaves, roots, shoots, and bark) and foods such as fruits, vegetables, nuts, oils, grains and grains. Bioactive compounds result from secondary plant metabolites and are not essential for their daily functioning, but play an important role in defense, attraction, signaling and competition and are therefore often referred to as secondary plant metabolites.

Types and main groups of bioactive compounds in vegetables

Bioactive compounds can be classified according to different criteria. The most commonly used classification in the literature is based on their pharmacological and toxicological effect. However, this is more relevant for clinicians, pharmacists or toxicologists and not for plant biologists, agronomists or other researchers involved in plant-related studies. For the latter groups, it is normal to classify them according to biochemical routes and chemical classes.

Example of health benefits of chemical classes
Vitamins

(C, E, and K) Antioxidant protection of cells and membranes against reactive oxygen species (ROS), protection of lipoproteins, stabilization of cell membrane structures, modulation of the immune response, inhibition of tumor growth in men. Fruits and vegetables. **Glycosides**

(Cardiac glycosides, cacogenic glycosides, glucosinolates, and anthraquinone glycosides) Recent reports provide a great deal of evidence about the chemo preventive role of different types of cancer glycosides (bladder, prostate, esophagus, and stomach) and degenerative cancer diseases. Glucosinolates, one of the most relevant groups of glycoside compounds, are capable of activating the enzymes involved in the detoxification of carcinogens, thus protecting against oxidative damage. Cruciferous vegetables, garlic, leek, onion.

Phenol

(Natural monophenols and polyphones, including phenol acids, flavonoids, aprons, chalconoids, flavonolignans, lingams, stableness, curcuminoids, and tannins) The specific effect of each phenol is difficult to assess because organisms absorb only a small part of it and can also undergo transformations. Epidemiological studies have claimed that polyphones can capture reactive oxygen species (ROS), inhibit per oxidation lipids on cell membranes, prevent LDL cholesterol from oxidizing and protect DNA from mutations and oxidations. Fruit and vegetables, tea, cocoa, wine, grapes, peanuts.

Arytenoids

(Arytenoids with provitamin an activity, which are vital components of the human diet) Although their bioactive mechanisms are still poorly understood, the importance of arytenoids for health is normally discussed in terms of antioxidant properties. Diets with many arytenoids are correlated with a significant reduction in the risk of certain cancers and cardiovascular and degenerative diseases. Epidemiological studies have shown that arytenoids can have anti-cancer and anti-mutagenic properties.

Green, orange, red and yellow vegetables.

Plant sterols

(Phytosterols) They regulate the fluidity and permeability of phospholipids double layers in plant membranes. Plant sterols are believed to have anticancer, anti-atherosclerotic, anti-inflammatory, and antioxidant activities.

Cruciferous vegetables, spinach, rice, soy, wheat germ, wheat bran, nuts, and vegetable seeds.

Alkaloids

(Morphine, cocaine, caffeine solacing) Morphine, cocaine, solacing, and caffeine are the most relevant alkaloids in plants. In addition to toxicity and their addictive effect, morphine and cocaine have been used in various formulations as anesthetics. Caffeine, the best-known alkaloid and in high concentrations, is toxic and protects plants against pests and vermin and prevents the germination of all other plants in the region (allopathic effects). Caffeine is also thought to reduce the risk of diabetes and heart disease in humans and has recently been associated with the prevention of Alzheimer's and Parkinson's disease. Papaveraceae (poppy family), coffee, cocoa, tea, Solanaceae (nightshade family), peppers, peppers, jalapeno eggplant, tomatoes, potatoes. Atop belladonna (deadly nightshade), Matura spp. (thorny apples). Spooning In addition to other properties, spooning are called cardio protective and hepatoprotective effects. Spooning has been shown to lower blood cholesterol levels, stimulate the immune system and inhibit the growth of cancer cells. Beans, cereals, chickpeas, oats, quinoa, asparagus, soy, red wine, and melons

Hydroponics and accumulation of bioactive compounds

Soil farmers experience the same types of variations in soil health and fluctuating environmental conditions. For example, water quality and variations in temperature and humidity can strain crops and possibly change their biochemical composition, regardless of the culture method used. Because of these variations, studies to date comparing the nutritional content of products grown in hydroponics with those produced in the soil have yielded mixed results, with some studies showing no difference between the two methods, while others show that aboveground systems performed better or worse than the ground. Grown controls in the tested nutrients. As you can imagine, the experimental design and conditions between these studies vary considerably and depend on the way they are designed and affect the outcome and meaning of the results. Several studies have claimed that hydroponic vegetables have better properties than those from conventional soil crops. On the other hand, other studies have confirmed that the exact differences between the qualities of vegetables grown in soil or hydroponics are difficult to establish. Nevertheless, all authors generally seem to agree that hydroponic systems can be the best alternative when arable land is scarce or their types are not ideal for the desired crop. Although there are different and conflicting opinions, the general opinion of the researcher seems to be that hydroponics can improve the content of bioactive substances. Recent studies have shown that with some high-quality fresh vegetables, hydroponic systems enable higher nutritional quality due to the high accumulation of bioactive compounds.

Premuzic et al. found an increase in macro and micronutrients and antioxidants in hydroponics, compared to soil-based production. Selma et al. found that the hydroponic system was more effective in controlling microbial contamination and higher antioxidant compounds, as this production method allowed for better maintenance of visual quality, tanning control and more effective in controlling microbial contamination. Compared to lettuce grown in soil. Pedneault et al. In Achilles mille folium found an accumulation of flavonoids in plants grown in hydroponics systems (0.43% dry weight) compared to plants grown in the field 0.38% dry weight). Besides, Sherri et al. found that the hydroponic culture of basil (Osmium basilica cv. Geneva) improved the antioxidant activity of aqueous and lipid extracts, thereby increasing the content of vitamin C, vitamin E, lipoid acid, total phenols, and rosemary acid.

Crop Results Reference

Basil Hydroponics has improved the levels of vitamin C, vitamin E, lipoid acid, total phenols, and rosmarinic acid, as well as their antioxidant activities.

The hydroponic salad offered yields 11 ± 1.7 times higher yields than conventionally produced but also required 82 ± 11 times more energy.

Lettuce the levels of alpha-tocopherol here were higher in hydroponics compared to conventional soil production.

Lettuce The content of lute in, beta-carotene, violaxanthin, and neoxanthin was lower in hydroponics compared to land-based production, due to less exposure of hydroponics to the sun and temperatures, which have a significant impact on carotenogenesis by lowering their levels. [6]

Lettuce grown in hydroponics had a considerably lower concentration of microorganisms than other lettuce grown in the soil.

Total onion flavonoids were comparable between hydroponics and soil-based crops.

> Red bell pepper The carotenoid content of capsorubin and capsanthin was higher in hydroponics (4.50 and 46.74 mg / 100 g dry weight, respectively) compared to conventional tillage (2.81 and 29.57 mg) / 100 g dry weight, respectively).

> The fruit yield of strawberries per plant was 10% higher in hydroponics raspberries than in raspberries grown in the soil.

> Sweet potato carotenes, ascorbic acid, thiamine, oxalic acid, and tannic acid and chymotrypsin and try sin inhibitors were higher in hydroponics.

> Tomato No significant difference between hydroponics and non-hydroponics tomatoes in

lycopene content (36.15 and 36.25 go / g, respectively). Tomato highly controlled conditions of electrical conductivity (EC) and salinity of water, pH and nutrients ensure optimum conditions for raising the levels of sugars, Bricks, pH and organic acids, quality criteria for consumer acceptance of tomatoes.

Comparative results between hydroponics and conventional soil production. Based on the results obtained by the different authors, it seems clear that they were all reported as common reasons for improving bioactive compounds in hydroponics - strict control of the entire breeding process, in particular, the amount and composition of nutrients and environmental conditions of temperature, humidity and light, and salinity of the water. Hydroponics operations, including water recirculation systems, can provide ideal conditions for the spread of secondary metabolites, especially when plants are under osmotic or salty stress, which stimulates the natural bioactive compounds of plants. Besides, the saturation of light and temperatures by leaf receptors, commonly used in these systems, helps to maximize photosynthesis and the subsequent production of carbohydrates that will be used for various biochemical mechanisms, including the biosynthesis of bioactive compounds, thereby increasing their content. For example, Greer and Weston [39] found that in a controlled environment with lower temperatures, anthocyanin levels in berries increased. Other authors have observed an increase in phenol acids, flavonoids and anthocyanins when the ratio of day/night temperature and day/night length changes from low to high. Also, a recent study [41] with rocket salads (Erica sativa, Erica vesicaria, and Diplotaxis tenuifolia) found that daytime lighting was long (16 hours of light, 8 hours of darkness) at an intensity of 200 mol m - 2 s -1, with daytime temperatures of 20 ° C and nighttime temperatures of 14 ° C, caused an increase in the content of polyphones and glucosinolates. Similarly, day/night temperatures and day/night length, nutrient solutions, type of light and CO_2 levels can be used to improve the bioactive compound content.

Food solutions with high electrical conductivity (EC) are effective in increasing lycopene (from 34 to 85%) in tomato cultivar. In a study with Genera bicolor DC (a traditional vegetable from China and Southeast Asia) subjected to 80% red light and 20% blue light, supplemented with an increase in CO_2 from 450 (ambient value) to 1200 mol - 1, the content bioactive compounds has been considerably improved. The anthocyanins and flavonoids content increased from 400 to 700 mg 100 g - 1 dry weight and from 250 to 350 mg 100 g - 1 dry weight, respectively. Therefore, growing plants in a highly controlled environment can be an effective alternative to maximize the production of bioactive compounds. Although hydroponics has many advantages over land production, several aspects should be taken into account when we decide to choose hydroponics. This type of production system requires regular irrigation and fertilization, which could otherwise lead to potential contamination of surface and groundwater. Besides, they required adequate management of pH, electrical conductivity (EC), dissolved oxygen and the temperature of nutrient solutions, as ionic concentrations can change over time, leading to unbalanced nutrients. That is why real-time and periodic measurements of nutrient solutions are necessary and adjustment of nutrient ratios is often necessary. Disinfection systems are also mandatory to prevent infections and diseases. All these aspects must be taken into account to achieve high quality without compromising production efficiency and safety.

Useful tips to improve your conversion rates Clones are very effective tools for reproducing your plants in your hydroponics project. You have to be extra careful to guarantee success; otherwise, you just waste time, energy and money. Here are some useful tips that can help you:

Clone only healthy, well-developed plants with improved flowering capacity.

Take more cuttings than you need to have a wider choice. Choose the best of them.

Before cutting, remove the nitrogen from the source plant by strongly feeding it for at least two and at most three days with water with an adjusted pH and without fertilizer or nutrient. If you do not do this, you will prevent the growth of the clone roots. Choose the medium that you want to use for your clones. You can use preformed cubes that contain holes suitable for cuttings. You have to make holes in the top of the support that has the same size or circumference as the stems of your clones. Be very careful when cutting Do not forget to sterilize your cutting equipment before cloning, as you could infect the mother plant. When cutting, make sure you do this quickly to prevent air from being thrown into the stem. The clone must be between three and six centimeters long - no more and no less. There must be at least one-page internodes and, if possible, two internodes. Place the cuttings in a misted dome where they are artificially hydrated two to three times a day. Also, keep them well ventilated by making small holes at the top of the dome. Keep their temperature at 72 degrees to 80 degrees Fahrenheit. Use double-tube fluorescent tubes that emit white light - cool and warm. Keep them close to the clones at a distance of one or two centimeters. If you use an artificial light system that uses metal halide or highpressure sodium lamps, keep the cuttings at a distance of two or three feet if the light source is. Between 175 and 400 watts. If the lamp power is at least a thousand, keep it at least four feet away; Keep the cuttings at least eighteen hours a day. Water the clones every other day with distilled water with nutrients. If the outside temperature is high, you can water them once a day. Do not make the mistake of submerging them or putting them in water, as the stems will rot or rot. Check the clones after about a week. If you see them begin to take root, stop misting or artificial hydration procedures. If they are already well-rooted, remove them from the dome and plant them.

Harvest: harden well

The right time to harvest your hydroponic garden When you have reached this stage, this means only one thing: you have completed the stages of growth and flowering of your plants. You have overcome the challenges of hydroponic gardening and triumphantly ignored the setbacks of raising your beloved fruits. The average harvest time is eight to twelve weeks of flowering. You must remember that they are best harvested when the production of trachoma's or the THC level is maximum. An indication of this is when at least a third of their pistils or hairs have gone from white to dark, such as brown or reddish. Use a magnifying glass to check the pistils. Do not wait too long until all the pistils are dark, as this will lower the value of your plants. Power and quantity are two non-parallel objectives when harvesting. If the first is your goal, you should harvest when the THC production is maximum and your harvested plants weigh less, but their quality would be much better. If the latter is your target, harvest them when all the pistils are dark.

Dry to improve quality

After harvesting, you must separate the leaves from the buds. The next step would be to dry and dry them. You must not forget that your leaves and buds leave a bad taste in the mouth and have a hard aroma when used or eaten immediately after harvest. They must be dried to remove or evaporate the water. The hardening step completes the drying process and completely transforms the leaves of your plants into carriers of good dreams and magic. Here are some things you should do when drying your plants:

Hang them in a dry, dark and cool environment. Keep the temperature at 20 degrees Celsius or 68 degrees Fahrenheit. Too much heat and light will destroy their quality. Do not touch the plants directly. Prevent damage to the quality of the buds, buds, and leaves by contaminating them with dirt or sweat from your hands. Separate large branches and larger leaves to allow smaller branches and narrower leaves to dry better. Keep the branches dry at a distance of half afoot. If they are too close together, your plants can attract mold; and when they are too far apart, they are dried faster than necessary. Both situations cause a loss of power and a decrease in quality. The average drying period is between one week and three weeks. To check whether your plants have dried up properly, take a few branches and fold them. If they break at an angle of 90 degrees or less, it means that your plants are already well dried. If they don't, you have to let them dry a little more.

The magic of healing

Curing is an important procedure in your horticultural project for hydroponics because they are responsible for converting your plants into salable quality products with high commercial value. Make sure you dry them well before you perform one of the hardening steps. Observe the following tips and you will certainly enjoy the triumph you have been waiting for:

Place your plants in airtight containers. Keep containers in an area where the temperature has stabilized at 20 degrees Celsius. Ensure that no light enters the room as this will damage the product. Any residual moisture in the contents of the sealed containers evaporates and adheres to the inner surface of the containers. Open the lids slowly and let the extra moisture escape. Do it during the first week with a twenty-four-hour interval for about thirty minutes.

Repeat the process during the second week with an interval of forty-eight hours. Repeat this during the third week and the following weeks if necessary until all condensation has been removed.

Beware of possible cavities caused by too much moisture. Signs of decay include a scent identical to that of compost and new grass residues.

Store dried plants that are no longer as green in airtight containers that must be placed in a place at a temperature of 20 degrees Celsius.

If you store them in a refrigerator, this could be a long way to prevent exposure to pollution, heat, and light, which could lead to deterioration in quality and a reduction in shelf life. Keep them intact for a few weeks or month

Prevention and eradication

Preventing and eradicating insects is one of the major concerns of hydroponic planters and agricultural scientists. With the advent of more scientific research and methods for studying bugs, modern science has developed innovative methods to prevent growth and prevent the existence of bugs. The Always clean your tools before and after using them.

1. Maintain proper drainage to ensure the cleanliness of the area.

2. Do not overwater because the unused water can become the haven of bugs.

3. Quarantine infected plants to prevent others from being infested too

Chapter 5

Hydroponics And Aerologic - Revolutions In Plant Cultivation

The agricultural revolution that has developed over the past year has made planting easier to consider than before. Hydroponics and aerologic are two breakthroughs, both of which have evolved considerably in the cultivation of agricultural and food products and have therefore contributed significantly to both individuals and economic growth. Hydroponics is the method for growing plants with nutrients dissolved in water. No soil is used for this process. The word hydroponics is derived from the Greek words hydro, which means water and pones, which means work. With the help of the hydroponics system, nutrients dissolved in water are supplied directly from their roots to plants. Geoponics is the method for growing plants in the air, it is a moist environment. Just like hydroponics, there is no use of soil in the aerologic system. The plants are grown in suspension in air and the nutrients are sprayed on the roots of the plants with a nutrient-rich water solution. The term geoponics is derived from the Greek words aero, which mean air, and pones, which means work. This happens in such a way that the mist is created in the air and there is no wind to move the mist away, the plants grow faster. The main difference between hydroponics and aerologic is the method for growing plants without soil. None of these methods requires soil for plant growth - the nutrients are supplied by a nutrient solution or a film whose formulation is sufficiently adapted to meet the requirements for sufficient plant growth. Many people are confused about agriculture and the difference between hydroponics and aerologic. Geoponics, in reality, a kind of hydroponic method for growing plants. It is water that supports the nutrient when the nutrient solution is sprayed into the roots of plants. Another major difference between hydroponics and aerologic is the environment in which plants are grown. When using the hydroponic method, plants are grown in a closed environment such as a greenhouse. Plants have grown using the aerologic method, but they are located in a closed or semi-closed area. Because the environment in which geoponics is used is not too limited and cultivated plants can become vulnerable to the risks of pests and diseases. When considering the difference between hydroponics and aerologic, it should be noted that plants grow faster with air because oxygen is abundant in combination with nutrient solution and water. Farmers prefer geoponics instead of hydroponics for growing plants, especially since geoponics ensures constant oxygen supply. This naturally translates into a much higher production yield than would be the case with hydroponics. Hydroponics and aerologic also differ in their configuration for plant growth. With geoponics, the method makes it possible to suspend the roots of plants in a hydro-atomized nutrient solution. As a result, parts of the plant roots extend over the top. Also, the aerologic method uses various technologies that can vary from a static solution to a continuous flow solution. Some care is also taken to prevent contamination by diseases in the irrigation system.

Despite the many differences between hydroponics and aerologic, it has undoubtedly been demonstrated that these two methods have an improved impact on the production of plants and food.

The hydroponics that is widely used nowadays

Hydroponics (from the Greek words hydro, water and pones, work), is a way for plants to grow in water, using solutions with mineral nutrients. The land is not used. Land plants can be grown with their roots only in the mineral nutrient solution or in an inert medium such as prelate, gravel, mineral wool or coconut husk. It was discovered in the 19th century that plants absorb mineral nutrients in the form of inorganic ions in water. Under natural conditions, and although the soil also acts as a reservoir of mineral nutrients, it is not per se relevant for plant growth. When the necessary mineral nutrients are artificially introduced into the water supply of a plant, the soil is not necessary for plant growth. Historically, hydroponics has been defined as the growth of crops in mineral nutrient solutions, without a solid medium for the roots. It is a subset of "above ground cultivation", which only requires that no clay or sludge soil is involved in the growth of the plants. Plants that are not generally grown in a natural environment can grow in a controlled climate system such as hydroponics. During World War II, products were grown in hydroponics on the dry Pacific island, and it was the first time that hydroponics was widely used to feed people. NASA has also attempted to use hydroponics in the space program. "Ray Wheeler, a plant physiologist at the Space Life Science Lab at the Kennedy Space Center, believes that hydroponics will advance space travel. He calls it" a life support system with the biological component of growing plants - called a regenerative life support system. It has several benefits for NASA. "These scientists are studying how different amounts of light, temperature, and carbon dioxide, as well as plant species, can be grown and grown on planets such as Mars. Hydroponics has taken plants growing to a whole new level and the methodology has even attracted those who have little interest in gardening or planting, but what are the pros and cons of hydroponics? There are several advantages to growing plants using the hydroponic method, which excludes the use of soil. The growing time is relatively much less and less space is needed. Moreover, it takes much less effort and requires less maintenance of the garden. Of course, it is also economical, because the water is preserved, the nutrients are recyclable and the problems of pests, weeds, and diseases are better controlled. There are no high parasites in the soil, productivity is higher and finally, control over the environment of the plant root has increased. Despite the advantages mentioned above, care must also be taken of the disadvantages of using hydroponic methods. These include fairly high installation costs and producers must have the right skills and knowledge to maintain maximum production in commercial applications. Although the threat of soil pests is absent, because every plant in a hydroponic system shares the same nutrient, pests and diseases can harm any plant. Besides, if there is an adverse climate change, hydroponic plants will wilt or shrink. Moreover, warm weather or reduced oxygen can delay production and lead to failed crops. We can, therefore, conclude that it is necessary to consider both the advantages and disadvantages of hydroponics. That is why we can make an informed decision so that you can make informed decisions about which application is suitable for the respective needs.

Famous hydroponics kits now

The hydroponic kit has all types of equipment needed to easily grow strong and healthy plants in your own home, with all the comfort and the right food to eat. Two Greek words were brought together to form hydroponics, "hydro" which means water and "pones" which means work that takes energy and time to consume your end product. And it is the work of hydroponics that makes vegetables use water and

.s all minerals to make food. Convection .dening is a mess in the area, but this method is ideal for people because it requires no soil and fertilization. Apart from the reduced clutter and the ability to grow plants in confined spaces, a hydroponic kit can also be adjusted and played as needed for your plants. People who are interested in gardening and planting in their own home and the first gardeners who want to switch from small gardening; the hydroponic kit is the best kit for them and for teaching them. The kit is equipped with all equipment and ingredients that will help you grow your green vegetables and other foods. Hydroponics is very useful for people in a recession where you can grow your plants and your food for a sustainable life. Hydroponics is mainly installed in kitchens so that they can be easily used and easily checked, such as herbs, fruits, vegetables, etc. When a kit is purchased, you receive the correct guidelines and instructions so that you can produce it correctly and without problems... For more guidelines, research on Google and other search engines can help you with your help in growing food.

Conclusion

Hydroponics is spreading around the world and such systems offer many new alternatives and opportunities for producers and consumers to make high-quality productions, including vegetables enriched with bioactive compounds. This chapter has provided a general overview of the role of hydroponics in improving these important types of non-essential nutrients, and based on the above discussion, hydroponics appears to be an essential tool for providing high-quality vegetables. Hydroponic and soil-based production systems, however, require good control and must be implemented correctly, taking full account of the needs of plants, soil, water, the environment, producers and consumer safety.

CPSIA information can be obtained
at www.ICGtesting.com
Printed in the USA
LVHW012048150621
690293LV00013B/1138

9 781802 030563